The Beautiful Word

100 ILLUSTRATED NIV SCRIPTURES
to NURTURE Your SPIRIT

by TAMA FORTNER

ZONDERVAN®

The Beautiful Word

Copyright © 2016 by Zondervan

Requests for information should be addressed to:
Zondervan, Grand Rapids, Michigan 49530

ISBN 978-0-7180-8819-4

Scripture quotations are taken from the Holy Bible, New International Version®, NIV®. Copyright © 1973, 1978, 1984, 2011 by Biblica, Inc.® Used by permission of Zondervan. All rights reserved worldwide. www.zondervan.com. The "NIV" and "New International Version" are trademarks registered in the United States Patent and Trademark Office by Biblica, Inc.®

Cover design: Connie Gabbert Design + Illustration
Interior design: Lori Lynch

Printed in China

16 17 18 19 20 / LEO / 22 21 20 19 18 17 16 15 14 13 12 11 10 9 8 7 6 5 4 3 2 1

To:

From:

The Beautiful Word

In the beginning there was only God, and then He spoke. Just a few words—and nothing became everything. Cold and empty void transformed into brilliant light and life. And the image of God was breathed into man, into woman, into us. All was beautiful, wondrous, and perfect.

And then came sin, sorrow, and separation—but then glorious hope. A Savior, a Seeker of souls, salvation! A bridge of forgiveness and relationship with God was purchased at a price beyond measure and made available to all who would believe. This eternal plan of salvation was designed by God from the very beginning.

IN the
beginning
God
created
the heavens
and the
earth

Genesis 1:1

What we deserve—oh, what we deserve!—for our sins and mistakes, for our stubbornness and pride, for our selfish and willful ways. But we are not given what we deserve. Instead, we are given grace: sweet, cleansing grace. We are neither cast away nor consumed because God's love and compassion never fail. Each morning dawns bright and new, fresh with potential and purpose, for the Lord faithfully washes away the confessed sins of our yesterday.

We deserve—oh, how we deserve—so much less, yet we are given infinite and unfailing *grace*.

Because of the *Lord's* great love we are not consumed, for his compassions never fail.

They are new every morning; great is your faithfulness.

Lamentations 3:22-23

"For I know the plans I have for you," declares the LORD. "plans to prosper you and not to harm you, plans to give you hope and a future. Then you will call on me and come and pray to me, and I will listen to you. You will seek me and find me when you seek me with all your heart."

Jeremiah 29:11–13

*P*lans—divinely promised and personal, beautifully crafted
by our Creator—for each one of us. Plans of hope, promise,
and a future.

How easily we find ourselves wandering through this
world, seeking which path to follow, trying first this one, then
that one. What wasted time, wasted strength. And all the while
the perfect plan—God's perfect plan—awaits us. We need only
to call out to the Lord in prayer, seek Him with all our heart,
and He is there with us. Holding us fast, lighting our way,
revealing to us—step by step—His perfect plan.

Now to him who is able to do immeasurably more than all we ask or imagine, according to his power that is at work within us.

· · ₒ ∘ ⟜ ≫ ✦ ≪ ⟞ ₃ ∘ ₒ ·

When we come before God with our hearts open, souls searching, and we ask, we plead, we seek, He answers. *Always.*

But do we ask enough? Are our prayers bold enough, our dreams big enough? For we do not come before some earthly king who is bound by the confines of time and space or wealth and power. We come before *Elohim*, the Almighty, the Creator and the Ruler of all that was and is and ever will be. Our God can and does do more—immeasurably more—than we could ever imagine. So *ask!* And then witness the wonders of God's glory revealed.

to **Him** who is *able* to do **IMMEASURABLY** **MORE** than all we ask or **IMAGINE.**

Ephesians 3:20

Whatever you do, work at it with all your heart, as working for the Lord, not for human masters.

W hatever we do—not just the grand and the great, not just the wonderful and the joyful, but *whatever* we do—we are to do with all our heart.

How easy it would be to become lazy, to let things slip, to offer up half-hearted efforts, especially to those who do not appreciate all that we give. But we are commanded and called to a greater purpose. We are reminded that our labors are not merely for man; they are for the One whose love for us was so great that He gave us His all. How, then, could we do any less than give Him ours?

your word is A lamp for my FEET, a light on my path.

Psalm 119:105

The Lord is Light, and His Word pierces through darkness to illuminate our way. Stepping out in faith, we set our feet upon the path with His precepts guiding us, protecting us. Darkness may swirl and threaten, but we do not worry. We cast away any fears, for darkness has no power or claim on those who walk in His light.

Trusting God with our all, we feast on the richness of His Word, tasting its sweetness and inscribing its promises upon the tablets of our minds and our hearts. The Lord is good; the Lord is faithful; the Lord is our Light.

*T*his Spirit of God, this part of Himself that dwells deep within us, is not a tiny spark, a mere flicker of light, or a dying ember. It is a flame, bright and burning, that is fanned by faith into a towering fire of courage, strength, and power. This fire is not of our own making, but of His as His courage, His strength, His power move in us and work through us.

The Spirit of God working within us burns away doubts, vanquishes fears, and wrestles worries to the ground, enabling us to stand brave, strong, and triumphant in the face of all that seeks to discourage us.

FOR THE
Spirit
GOD GAVE US DOES
NOT MAKE US TIMID,
BUT GIVES US

power,

love

AND

self-discipline.

2 TIMOTHY
1:7

THEREFORE,

ANYONE IS IN
CHRIST,
THE NEW
CREATION
HAS COME:

HAS GONE,
THE NEW
HERE!

2 CORINTHIANS 5:17

We are rescued! We are redeemed from our sins! The ransom was paid by One who did not owe. We are reconciled to God by our Savior's sacrifice and a love so great that we can only glimpse its depths.

And the magnitude of our debt? Beyond measure, considering the great cost paid. Yet such grace is never to be repaid but ever to be reflected in the words and the steps of people living lives of humble gratitude.

Old ways are swept away; old sins, forgotten; old lives, gone. We are a new creation, glorious and shining, bought by the blood of Christ and made new by the very hands of God.

Ever growing, ever changing, ever drawing nearer to Him, we are ever being beautifully and wonderfully transformed into the image of our Savior. Believing that Jesus is Lord and embracing His call upon our lives, we offer to those around us the goodness, the kindness, the love with which He has graced us.

And as our knowledge of who He is grows, may we allow Him to mold our character. May we also become more determined to follow Jesus, to live as He lived, to love as He loved. For our Lord is love, and in loving others, we reveal that we are His.

For this very reason, make every effort to add to your faith goodness; & to goodness, knowledge; & to knowledge, self-control; & to self-control, perseverance; & to perseverance, godliness; & to godliness, mutual affection; & to mutual affection, love.

2 PETER 1:5-7

Seek God.

Before we seek to serve or to please others, before we seek to serve or to please ourselves, before we seek to serve or to please the world—we are to seek Him. And seeking Him means setting aside worries, casting away fears, and searching out the path that the One who made us, who loves us, and who redeems us wants us to walk. We trust His guidance, knowing the Lord cares for His own.

Our heavenly Father's promised provision is celebrated in the sparrow's sweet song, and His love is reflected in the attire of the lilies. We trust that He who watches over the birds and the flowers watches over us. And as we seek Him, we find life-sustaining joy, hope, and peace.

BUT SEEK FIRST HIS KINGDOM AND HIS RIGHTEOUSNESS, AND ALL THESE THINGS WILL BE GIVEN TO YOU AS WELL. [MATTHEW 6:33]

till. Was there ever such hope, such joy, such a priceless treasure? Not after we pulled ourselves up to some false pretense of perfection, but *while we were still sinners*, Christ died for us.

Our Lord did not come to redeem those who did not need Him; He came to redeem the lost, the mixed-up and messed-up, the crippled, and the imprisoned—all waiting for the glorious power of His salvation to be set free.

So much love, so much mercy, and so much grace for us who were *still* sinners.

BUT GOD DEMONSTRATES
HIS OWN LOVE FOR US IN THIS:

*While
we were still
sinners,
Christ died
for us.*

Romans 5:8

"Have I not commanded you? Be strong and courageous. Do not be afraid; do not be discouraged, for the Lord your God will be with you wherever you go."

Courage and fear, strength and weakness—they war within us, battling for control. Doubt and discouragement lay siege to our thoughts and our hearts, seeking to starve away faith and hope, to overpower light with darkness. But those enemies do not win—can never win—because He who is within us is greater than any who would attack us.

The Lord our God fights for us—and, yes, it is a battle, but a battle He has already won. So we fling away fear, clothe ourselves in His strength, and anchor our faith on His promises—for the Lord is with us wherever we go!

I AM WHO I AM.

EXODUS 3:14

God said to Moses, "I AM WHO I AM. This is what you are to say to the Israelites: 'I AM has sent me to you.'"

Who is the One calling to hearts and seeking souls, wanting to lift away sins and heal with tender mercies? It is the I AM. There is no other; there can be no other. There is only the great and glorious I AM, Ruler of all eternity, sovereign Lord, Jehovah God. *I AM!*

His name is forever. It does not change, for He does not change. He is the one true God who called Abraham, who delivered Isaac, and who led Jacob. And He is the one true God who calls us, delivers us, and leads us.

The greatest of gifts ever given—unearned and utterly undeserved—is salvation for our souls, purchased at a price we could never pay. This gift? It is the grace of God.

Bought with blood, secured by sorrow, and redeemed by the Savior's resurrection, this grace of God is priceless and precious, yet freely given to all who simply open their hearts, minds, and souls to receive it. Once accepted, grace sweeps away the hopelessness of the eternity we deserve and gifts us instead with the glories of heaven. Oh, the sweet, saving, amazing grace of God!

Enemies surround and battles rage. Days are filled with strife and struggle. And our reaction, our response, is to fight, to swing, to sling, to do something . . . *anything.* But the Lord—He who sees our battles, knows our weaknesses, senses our deepest fears—says to our warring hearts, "Be still, and know that I am God" (Psalm 46:10).

The Lord of heaven's armies is with us. Our almighty God is our strength and our shield. We have no need to fear or to fight, for He fights for us!

Lord, the God of Israel, there is no God like you in heaven or on earth—you who keep your covenant of love with your servants who continue wholeheartedly in your way.

Amazing and almighty God, King of all creation—He alone is worthy of praise and adoration. Nothing compares to His majesty in the heavens above or on the earth below. His promise of love is ours to claim from this very moment through all of eternity. He fills our souls with hope, chases away darkness, and illuminates our way.

When we stumble on this earthly path, when the uncertainties of this world overwhelm us, He reaches down, lifts us up, and invites us to breathe deeply of His presence. He reassures . . . renews . . . restores . . . redeems.

LORD, THE GOD of ISRAEL, there is no God like you in HEAVEN or on EARTH— YOU WHO KEEP YOUR covenant of LOVE

2 CHRONICLES 6:14

he heals the BROKENHEARTED AND BINDS up THEIR wounds. Psalm 147:3

The Lord sees.

The world may turn away from us, brushing aside our sorrow, suffering, and pain. But the Lord sees. He who numbers the very hairs on our heads knows our every heartache, hears our anguished cries, aches with us at our every wound, sees each tear that falls. This compassionate and gracious God stops to record each trouble, to capture each tear.

And then the great *El Roi*, the One who sees, pulls us close, holds us near. He heals heartaches, binds wounds, wipes away tears, and softly whispers to us sweet truths: *We are loved. We are seen. We are His.*

the
LORD
your
GOD
goes
with
you;
he
will
never
LEAVE
you
NOR
forsake
you.

DEUTERONOMY 31:6

Be strong and courageous. Do not be afraid or terrified
because of them, for the LORD your God goes with you;
he will never leave you nor forsake you.

A lone . . . utterly and completely alone.

The fear of it steals our breath, clutches at our heart, haunts our dreams. No one to help us; no one to comfort us.

Yet *alone* is something we need never be, for God makes us a promise—a great and mighty promise that uplifts, strengthens, reassures. It brings light and hope to the darkest night and to the bleakest day. Wherever we go, He is there *with* us, always and forever. Never does He leave us, never does He forsake us. We are never alone!

aith is not fleeting; faith is fierce. Faith boldly believes the unwavering promises of God. And faith is ours to choose, ours to have. That faith grows because we know—*we know* and we see—that the Lord is faithful. His faithfulness echoes through the ages, through Noah and Abraham, Sarah and Hannah, and continues to this day.

So while we do not yet see God face-to-face, we see the glory of His very real mercy and grace in our own lives. Confident, assured, and daily reassured, we believe because of faith.

NOW FAITH IS CONFIDENCE IN WHAT WE HOPE FOR & ASSURANCE ⟩⟩⟩⟩⟩⟩ ABOUT WHAT WE DO NOT SEE.

HEBREWS 11:1

Dear Children, let us not **LOVE** with words or speech but with Actions and in Truth.

1 JOHN 3:18

Love is more—so much more—than sentimental words without substance. Love is no mere misty-eyed feeling; it is getting up and doing. It is seeing a need and rising to meet that need, giving of what we have to those who have not. Love is hands reaching to help and hearts risking heartache to befriend and comfort those who are lonely and hurting.

Comfortable, easy, without cost—that is not love. Love is sacrifice, one for another. Love is a life laid down in service, in gratitude, to the One who loved enough to lay down His life for us.

But now, for a brief moment, the LORD our God has been gracious in leaving us a remnant and giving us a firm place in his sanctuary, and so our God gives light to our eyes and a little relief in our bondage.

Sometimes we forget. We forget to remember the Lord and His love, His promises and His unending faithfulness. We often forget Him, even flee from Him, in the rush and whirl of selfish, busy lives. But even though we forget Him, He remains with us. His still, small voice is ever stirring within our hearts the remnant of His Word—that remnant that ever lingers deep within our souls.

And when we remember Him, when we return to Him, His mercy sweeps away our transgressions and renews our spirits. And He welcomes us—forgetful, wandering sinners washed clean—into the sweet sanctuary of His grace.

BUT NOW, FOR A BRIEF MOMENT, the Lord our God HAS BEEN GRACIOUS IN LEAVING US A REMNANT AND GIVING US A FIRM PLACE IN HIS SANCTUARY.

EZRA 9:8

A light to the world: that is what Jesus called us to be. We are to reflect God's goodness and His grace, His gentle kindness and His fierce love. We are to chase away darkness and point the way to hope and peace for a world weary of and weary from its struggles. But not all who live in darkness will welcome the light.

So to shine—to boldly proclaim the news of Jesus' forgiveness and love, to not hide the light of His truth in the shadows of our fear—is to risk, to dare. Yet for this very purpose we were made: to shine into the darkness of the world the life-giving, life-changing light of the Lord.

TRUST

in the

LORD WITH ALL YOUR

heart

AND LEAN NOT ON YOUR OWN UNDERSTANDING;
IN ALL YOUR WAYS SUBMIT TO HIM,
& HE will make your

paths

STRAIGHT.

Proverbs 3:5-6

To reach out, to slip a hand into His, to place a heart in His keeping—*that* is trusting the Lord. He is our greatest comfort, our greatest strength, and our greatest hope. We give over to Him all that is within us, completely surrendering our will without worry or fear, knowing that He will care for us because we are His beloved ones.

Our trust is God's great treasure. And with that trust held close to His heart, He works in our lives to guide, to shield, and to straighten the path before us—drawing us closer, ever closer, to Him.

· · · · ● ● ● · · ·

"Go!" Jesus commanded. And because we have been forgiven for our sins, because we have been blessed with the promise of eternal life, because we have been told to, we go.

We go and give to those who hunger and thirst for food—and for righteousness. We go into a world wrapped in cold darkness and share the warming Light of love, hope, and promises more certain than the sun. We go and tell the good news, the glorious news of Christ, of Jesus, of God's own Son: He is risen, He is alive, and He is seeking to save the lost. And because we are His, we go!

therefore GO and MAKE disciples OF ALL NATIONS.

Matthew 28:19

As for God, his way is perfect: The LORD's word is flawless;
he shields all who take refuge in him.

F lawless and unerring Truth, unfailing and unfaltering Love—that is our Lord, and no wonder His way is perfect.

To take refuge in Him is to have darkness become light, fear become faith, and weakness become strength. For He stands between us and that which would harm us.

And when we choose Him—when we cease our strivings, our useless attempts to save ourselves—He shields us. But much more than shielding us, He arms us, prepares us for the battle, and makes our way secure. The Lord is our Refuge when we choose Him.

THE LORD'S word is FLAWLESS;

HE SHIELDS ALL who TAKE refuge IN HIM.

2 SAMUEL 22:31

But he said to me, "My *grace* is sufficient for you, for my power is made perfect in weakness." Therefore I will boast all the more gladly about my weaknesses, so that Christ's *power* may rest on me.

2 Corinthians 12:9–11

*T*houghts stumble heavenward, rising from heavy hearts and struggling spirits. Our prayers—*Why, God? Please, Lord. This is too much!*—are pleas for grace, peace, and hope.

And our Father, ever faithful and true to His promises, gathers us into the sweet shelter of His arms. Holding us close, clutching us near to His heart, He whispers, *This weakness I will use.* For in our weakness we lean into His strength, and then by His power, we do that which we alone could not have done.

Everlasting love and unfailing kindness are precious gifts from God. By His hand, sorrow is turned to joy, mourning into gladness. By His hand, we are delivered from those who would harm us; by His grace, we are gathered from the wilderness of this world; and by His mercy, our souls are restored, made holy and whole.

We walk beside peaceful waters, and we do not stumble because of the Lord: He loves with an everlasting love and blesses with His unfailing kindness.

I have loved you
with an
everlasting love;
I have drawn you with unfailing kindness.
Jeremiah 31:3

For in him we *live* and move & have our *being.*

Acts 17:28

What inexpressible, indescribable joy: to live and to move and to *be* because of God! Our every moment, every movement, and every breath is sustained by Him. Our thoughts directed to Him are precious reminders that we depend upon the Lord who listens and who loves us always.

Breathe in the fragrance of Him—sweeter than any rose, softer than any summer breeze—for He is our Lord. He is the essence of love and hope, light and life. And surrendering to Him means peace, joy, and rest for world-weary souls. In Him, we are beloved children who are adored, sought after, and saved.

Being confident of this, that he who began a good work in you will carry it on to completion until the day of Christ Jesus.

We seek to do right, and still so often we do wrong. We struggle against selfish, self-seeking sin, sometimes winning and other times . . . not. Guilt haunts and doubts assail, and we cannot help but wonder, even worry, *Is the Lord's grace enough? Is His love enough for such stumbling ones was we?*

And His answer—swift, certain, and sure—is yes: *My grace is sufficient. And I will always love you.*

We are saved by the blood of Christ; we are delivered from the consequences of our sin because of His death and resurrection. Still we stumble and sin; we are far from being perfect reflections of Jesus' image. Yet we are—by God's grace— wondrous works in process, molded by the hands of the great Creator.

HE WHO BEGAN A *Good work in you* will carry it on to COMPLETION until the day of *Christ Jesus*

Philippians 1:6

YOU will KEEP IN perfect PEACE those WHOSE minds ARE STEADFAST, because THEY TRUST in you.

ISAIAH 26:3

eace. Heaven-perfected peace. And peace on earth, not held in heaven alone. Peace with God offered to all, lasting through eternity. Offered to all who fix their hearts and minds steadfast upon the Savior: to those experiencing the gale-force winds of the world, to those who choose to trust in the midst of such storms, to those who stand unfalteringly and firmly on the Word, on the promises of God.

Because no matter the storms that threaten, no matter the winds that blow, we know the Lord is faithful. His promises are true. We are loved. We are shielded. We are saved!

The Vine, our Lord and our Redeemer, is the Source of life, the Source of our strength. His Spirit courses within us, extending springs of hope into our hearts, our souls. The Spirit transforms us and renews us, enabling us to sink our roots deep into His divine truth and His unending love.

Staying attached to the Vine, we find our purpose and our calling. And stay attached we must, for to be broken off from Him is to wither. Connected to the Vine, we are made whole, and we bear the beautiful fruit of salvation. Life, light, and joy—eternal and everlasting—are found only in the Vine, in our Savior, the Christ.

ALWAYS
BE
PREPARED TO GIVE
AN
ANSWER TO
EVERYONE
WHO
ASKS
YOU TO GIVE
THE REASON
FOR
THE HOPE THAT
YOU
HAVE.
>>>>>>>>
1 PETER 3:15

In your hearts revere Christ as Lord. Always be
prepared to give an answer to everyone who asks
you to give the reason for the hope that you have.
But do this with gentleness and respect.

Why? the world questions. *Why believe in the Lord?*
Why put faith in His promises and live in obedience to His
commands? *Why believe in One who cannot be seen?* And for the
world's questions, we must have an answer. But we must have
an answer not only for the world but also for ourselves.

Why?

We have hope because God has made His great love known
to us. We have hope because we have seen His faithfulness. And
we live for Him because He chose to die for us.

He has shown you, O mortal, what is good. And what does the
LORD require of you? To act justly and to love mercy and to
walk humbly with your God.

What shall we give the Lord who gave His all for us? What could we—mere mortals, sinful creatures—give to our almighty, holy God? After all, everything we have, everything that is good, comes from Him; everything is already His. Every animal of the forest, every creature of the sea, every bird of the air is His. All the earth is His—all wealth and power, honor and glory. What could we possibly give Him?

We—who are His too—give what He asks: we surrender our hearts, minds, and souls. We choose to love God by doing acts of justice and mercy as His representatives. And knowing His Word and seeking His will, we humbly let Him guide our steps.

TO
ACT *justly*
AND TO
LOVE *mercy*
AND TO
WALK *humbly*
WITH YOUR
GOD.

MICAH 6:8

The Lord searches every *heart* & understands every desire & every thought.

1 Chronicles 28:9

There are no secrets before the Lord. Nothing is concealed. Not one thing is hidden. He knows *all*: every wayward thought, every darkened desire, every silenced sin. And yet He still loves, still cherishes, still seeks to save us. So He waits.

He waits for the one word, for the searching heart, for the heaven-turned hope, and then He gently makes His presence known. *Seek and find*—this is the promise, made long ago and still offered today, the promise kept always. No, no secrets are hidden . . . and no seeking souls are denied.

God is not some distant deity, not some uncaring king or self-serving sovereign. He is instead our Father. *Abba*. A name above any other name, hallowed and holy. His kingdom is beyond our greatest imaginings; His will, perfect and eternal; His love and care for us, without end. *Abba*, our Father.

How can we pray to One so great, so grand? We pray as a child, lifting up our hearts and hands and voices to Him—to our heavenly Father who reaches down to lift us up into His arms.

Forgive us, guide us, shield us, and protect us from the one who would destroy us, oh Father in heaven, our *Abba* God.

OUR FATHER IN
HEAVEN,
HALLOWED BE YOUR NAME,
YOUR KINGDOM COME,
YOUR WILL BE DONE,
ON EARTH AS IT IS IN
HEAVEN.
GIVE US TODAY OUR
DAILY BREAD.
AND FORGIVE US OUR DEBTS,
AS WE ALSO HAVE FORGIVEN OUR
DEBTORS.
AND LEAD US NOT INTO
TEMPTATION,
BUT DELIVER US FROM THE
EVIL ONE.

MATTHEW 6:9-13

do not be
anxious
about anything,
but in every situation, by
PRAYER & PETITION,
with
thanksgiving,
PRESENT YOUR
requests to God.

PHILIPPIANS 4:6

Sometimes our prayer is simply a breath. We exhale the worries and wonders and restless wanderings of our lives and place them in God's hands. Then we inhale the provision and the promises and the peace of the Almighty. We let go to just *be* with God and to breathe in His presence.

Every anxious thought, every care, every burden, every fear—we lay all these down before His throne. No need to carry them any longer, any further. For the Lord hears our every prayer; He knows our every need. May we simply believe, pray, and breathe.

WE HAVE THIS HOPE AS AN ANCHOR FOR THE SOUL, FIRM AND SECURE.

Never moving, never shaken, never changing is the Lord, our Anchor. He holds us fast and keeps us secure, safely moored in the sheltered cove of His promised hope.

And that hope—the hope we have in Him—is real. It is not some shimmering, wished for, dreamed of, once-upon-a-time fairy-tale hope. The hope God offers is a promise, certain and sure. His is a promised hope that reached up from the cross to rend the temple curtain that separated us from Him, ushering us safely into the sanctuary of God's presence.

WE HAVE this hope as an ANCHOR for the soul.

HEBREWS 6:19

A gentle ANSWER TURNS AWAY wrath, BUT A harsh word & STIRS UP anger.

PROVERBS 15:1

How words can slice and sting! Piercing and sharp, they cut away at our sense of self, our security, our worth. Our reply waits, bitter and bold, on our tongue poised to strike, to lash out, to exact vengeance. And yet . . .

We know this is not to be our way, for it is not the way of the Lord. So we bite back the harshness, swallow the anger and pride, and—in His power—offer gentler, kinder words instead. Words of love and grace, of hope and healing. For such are the words He offers us.

We have been lifted out of slavery, with our bonds broken and chains cast away. Neither the pharaohs of old nor the sins of today can lay claim to us, for our freedom has been purchased because of a love that is beyond understanding. This love is our gift from God.

And to Him and Him alone we bow down, surrendering hearts, minds, and souls. To Him alone we offer up the praise of our lives, our days, our lips, our hands, our feet. For there is no other god: there is only Yahweh. To Him alone be glory, honor, and dominion forever and always. Amen.

the Ten Commandments

"YOU SHALL HAVE NO OTHER GODS BEFORE ME.

You shall not make for yourself an image
in the form of anything in heaven above
or on the earth beneath or in the waters below.

YOU SHALL NOT MISUSE THE NAME OF
THE LORD YOUR GOD.

Remember the Sabbath day by keeping it holy

Honor your father and your mother.

YOU SHALL NOT MURDER.

You shall not commit adultery

YOU SHALL NOT STEAL.

You shall not give false testimony
against your neighbor.

YOU SHALL NOT COVET...
anything that belongs to your neighbor."

EXODUS 20:2-17

Praise be to the God and Father of our Lord Jesus Christ,
the Father of compassion and the God of all comfort.

When the storms have been too strong, too many, or too harsh, we seek comfort—comfort for that aching need deep within our souls, that need for a gentle word, a loving touch, the reassurance that somehow, someday all will be well. Human arms can hold and human words can heal, yet only incompletely.

But there is One who holds, who heals, who loves, and who comforts *completely.* We can run to the heavenly Father, close our troubled eyes, nestle in, and breathe deeply of His presence and His care. May the God of compassion comfort us as we find rest in Him.

the *Father* of compassion & THE *God* of all comfort.

2 CORINTHIANS 1:3

let us not become weary in doing GOOD, FOR at the PROPER time we will REAP a harvest if we DO NOT give UP.

Galatians 6:9

The goodness of God sweetens our lives and saves our souls. And the goodness of God should guide our words, our steps, our days. But when the world laughs at faith, when those we seek to help scorn and scoff, we find it easy to grow weary, to give up, to retreat within ourselves. But we cannot allow it to be so.

After all, Christ Himself was mocked and scorned. Should we as His followers expect anything less? And still Jesus did not grow tired, did not weary of doing good. Should we do any less, by His power and for His glory?

Let everything that has breath praise the Lord. Praise the Lord.

PSALM 150:6

*P*raise the Lord! Let everything that lives and moves and breathes praise the Lord, for He is King of all creation, Lord above all lords.

The lion lies down before His throne, the lamb finds shelter in His shadow, and the eagles soar upon the winds of His might. Stars bow from the heavens, and the oceans ring out their praises.

And we—children of His hope and His salvation—lift our hands high, open our hearts wide, and sing praises to the Lord most high. Hallelujah! Praise to our King! Praise to our God!

> Though one may be overpowered, two can defend themselves. A cord of three strands is not quickly broken.

One walks alone, unguarded and easily lost. Two walk together, stronger than one, yet still vulnerable. But three who walk in step? Three stand strong, especially when the third is the Savior. For where two or more are gathered in His name, He is there in might and in majesty.

Tensions twist, struggles strain, and worries work to wrench us apart, but the cord of three strands—a cord woven together, bound together, with fellowship and with the Savior's love—it holds. It is not broken; *we* are not broken. Through His power, we hold strong.

A

CORD OF

THREE

STRANDS

IS

NOT

QUICKLY

BROKEN.

ECCLESIASTES 4:12

Every good and perfect gift is from above, coming down from the Father of the heavenly lights, who does not change like shifting shadows.

The Lord our God is good, and He blesses us—His beloved children—with His goodness. In Him is no darkness; only light. No evil or temptation; only glory and honor. No falsehood or fear; only truth and love.

He is the Father of light, and unlike the shifting shadows of the father of lies, our God does not change. The Lord's promises are ever true, steadfast, and sure. Hope and joy, love and grace, every good and perfect gift—all are given by our faithful Father.

A song rings through the heavens with notes pure and clear. It echoes beyond the stars and fills eternity with joy. It is the boundless, endless song of our Lord, and it is for us—the chosen, the called, the children of God.

His voice, rich and sure, flows over our souls, soothing and reassuring us. Dangers may assail, enemies may attack, but we do not cower; we do not fear. For the Lord God is with us. Our mighty Warrior, He saves us, He delights in us, and, rejoicing, He sings over us!

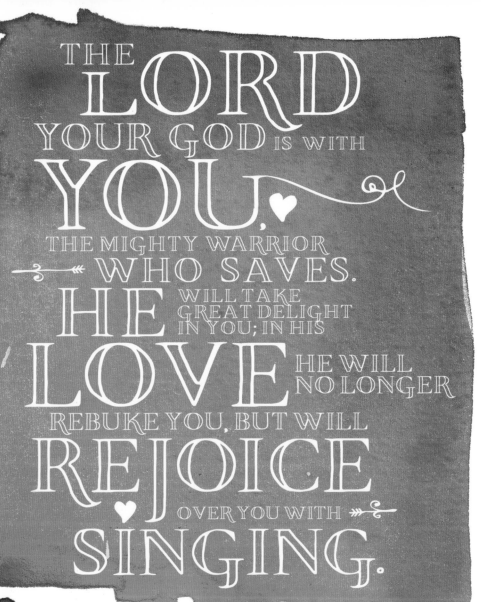

THE **LORD** YOUR GOD IS WITH **YOU,** THE MIGHTY WARRIOR WHO SAVES. **HE** WILL TAKE GREAT DELIGHT IN YOU; IN HIS **LOVE** HE WILL NO LONGER REBUKE YOU, BUT WILL **REJOICE** OVER YOU WITH **SINGING.**

ZEPHANIAH 3:17

For God so loved. These simple words hold so much—so much hope, so much joy, so much promise . . . so much love.

How great the gift we are given, that the Father would offer up His Son for our salvation, would seek out sin-filled souls to make His own. And the Son, such sacrifice so willingly made: the stripes, the thorns, the agony, and the shame He bore—all for us, that we might be welcomed as God's children.

Loved—so tiny, so humble a word to contain the immeasurable grace the Lord has offered.

FOR GOD SO Loved THE WORLD THAT HE GAVE HIS ONE & ONLY SON, THAT WHOEVER BELIEVES IN HIM SHALL not perish BUT HAVE ETERNAL LIFE.

JOHN 3:16

Our words, when lifted to the Lord, become so much more—infinitely more—than mere words. Soft syllables of spoken faith, whispered words of time-tested trust and bold belief. Community strengthened by carrying each other's burdens. Hopes turned heavenward and made holy by the One who listens, who hears, and who answers.

With words, we step into the very throne room of heaven, into the very presence of God. With words, we lay bare our souls, unshoulder our burdens, and seek mercy and grace, for ourselves and for others. And with words, we curl into the arms of our Father, lay our head upon His shoulder, and find sweet peace. That is the power of prayer.

CONFESS YOUR SINS to each other AND pray for each other SO THAT YOU MAY BE HEALED. The prayer of a RIGHTEOUS PERSON IS powerful AND effective.

James 5:16

you
make known
to me
the path
of life.

Psalm
16:11

You make known to me the path of life; you will fill me with joy in your presence, with eternal pleasures at your right hand.

Decisions, choices, what-ifs—these circle and swirl and whirl through our minds, clouding our vision like a thick fog.

As we face a fork in the road, we wonder and we wander until at last we remember the One who knows the way. Once we remember the Lord our God, we lift up our hands, seeking His wisdom and guidance, seeking Him: *Which way, God? Which way?*

And He—Lord of all, Master of all—He takes our hand, soothes our troubled brow, and gently whispers, *This way. No . . . not that way. This way. This way is the path of life.*

The word of God is alive and active. Sharper than any double-edged sword, it penetrates even to dividing soul and spirit, joints and marrow; it judges the thoughts and attitudes of the heart.

The Lord our God is alive! And He speaks to us through the Word of truth that gives us life eternal. Far more than mere words upon a page, God's Word works in our hearts and out into the very moments of our lives.

With silvery sharpness, it slices like a sword through the delusions and illusions the evil one uses to deceive and destroy—even through the lies we tell ourselves. Pure truth and a refining fire, God's Word burns through to the essence of who we are and reveals who the Lord created us to be.

the word of GOD is ALIVE & ACTIVE. HEBREWS 4:12

"This is what the Sovereign LORD says: I myself will search for my sheep and look after them."

The Lord God is the Almighty, the Author of all history and Ruler of all the vastness and wonders of creation. No world can contain His presence, no words can fully describe Him, no mind can grasp His might, and yet . . . and *yet* . . . He stoops down from the stars to shepherd us, His sheep.

When we wander, He searches for us and seeks until He finds us. When we are wounded, He comforts, soothes, restores. Always our loving Shepherd, He guides us to sweet pastures, fills our hearts with song, and strengthens our souls. Tender and watchful, the Lord our Shepherd looks after us and leads us home.

I MYSELF
will search for my sheep and look after them.

EZEKIEL 34:11

If serving the LORD seems undesirable to you, then choose for yourselves this day whom you will serve, whether the gods your ancestors served beyond the Euphrates, or the gods of the Amorites, in whose land you are living. But as for me and my household, we will serve the LORD.

We live with a seemingly endless barrage of choices. Their sheer numbers threaten to overwhelm us. But that won't happen—that can't happen—because choices are not endless. Not at all. Our choices are only two: choose the Lord and His way or choose . . . the other.

And choose we must, for there is no halfway, no straddling, no compromise. With every word spoken, every step taken, every thought harbored, we choose either to honor or to deny God. We choose between love and hate, truth and lies, hope and despair. We choose between being found and being lost, between life and death. Choose life! Choose the Lord!

but as
FOR ME
AND MY
household
WE WILL
serve the
LORD.

JOSHUA 24:15

Do not conform to the pattern of this world, but be transformed by the renewing of your mind. Then you will be able to test and approve what God's will is—his good, pleasing and perfect will.

Transformation—the process begins with believing and continues until we see our God face-to-face, until we hear His "Well done." Such a life is a breath-stealing, soul-saving, sin-defying adventure with the One who loves us, who wants more for us. It requires a deep-water dive into the Word of God, allowing it to penetrate us, renew us, and remake us from the inside out.

Sometimes painful and frightening, always radical and renewing, transformation is the power of God at work in our lives, molding and shaping us into the image of His one and only Son.

do not conform
to the pattern of this world,
but be transformed
by the renewing of your mind.

Romans 12:2

Hear, O Israel:

The Lord our God, the Lord is one.

Love the Lord your God with all your heart and with all your soul and with all your strength. These commandments that I give you today are to be on your hearts. Impress them on your children. Talk about them when you sit at home and when you walk along the road, when you lie down and when you get up. Tie them as symbols on your hands and bind them on your foreheads.

Deuteronomy 6:4-8

*H*ear, O Israel: the Lord our God is good, gracious, and glorious! His power is infinite, and His presence is all-encompassing. And this God—who is with us, for us, and even deep within us—loves us with a love that stretches beyond eternity.

Let the truth of His love be written upon our hearts, our souls, our lives—for all the world to read. Let others open up the books of our lives and see written upon our pages the very presence of God. And because we love, let others believe that God loves.

WHATEVER **YOU DID** FOR ONE OF THE **LEAST OF** THESE BROTHERS & SISTERS OF MINE, **YOU DID FOR ME.**

MATTHEW 25:40

"The King will reply, 'Truly I tell you, whatever you did for one of the least of these brothers and sisters of mine, you did for me.'"

>>>

A cup of water, a bit of bread, a few moments of our day—such simple offerings to one in need are also offerings to the One above. For the hand that takes hold of the cup we extend is the hand of heaven. The shoulders that shiver are our Savior's. And the eyes that weep? They weep the tears of Christ.

These hurting ones, these hungry and thirsty ones, these sheep in need of the Shepherd—they are known by Him. He knows their every sorrow and pain, and He sees every comfort we offer in His name. For our gift to them is our gift to Him.

God is gracious, and He lavishes us—so undeserving, yet so very grateful—with His grace. A grace that erases past mistakes, soothes godly sorrows, and whispers, *I, the Lord your God, forgive you.*

And why so great a gift for us who deserve punishment and death? Because God sees us—His beloved children, burdened by our sin, walking in darkness, living apart from Him—and His heart fills with tender compassion. He sees our struggles and understands our temptations because He has walked on this planet. Because His Son became flesh and faced all that we face and infinitely more. The Lord did not come to condemn, but to offer compassion that acts to restore, guide, embolden . . . to offer unlimited compassion born of boundless love.

I knew that you are a

Gracious & Compassionate God,

slow to anger & abounding in love, a God who relents from sending calamity.

Jonah 4:2

*W*ithout love, there is only the cold, unyielding darkness, void of hope, of joy, of purpose. Without love, there is *nothing*. But . . .

There *is* love! And it's the Lord's love, rich and warm and bright, overflowing with hope, radiant with joy, and blessing His children with His purpose: to love Him and to love others in response to His love. To love without asking, without demanding, without limit. To create sweet sanctuary, a safe shelter where souls can heal. To offer a gentle touch, a forgiving way. To treasure, to honor, and to cherish those hearts entrusted to us. We love others as He has loved us.

To follow the Lord's example, to live as Christ lived, to walk in the way of love as He did is a bold and daring choice. It is one foot placed determinedly in front of the other, sometimes steady, sometimes uncertain. But still moving forward, still sharing simple kindnesses and gentle words, still daring to love.

Yes, Jesus' way involves risk. The path is often pitted and marred, and there are those who would trip us up just to watch us fall. Still, we follow Jesus' path. *Why?* the world wonders. And our answer? We are children of our heavenly Father, dearly loved by Him, and walking in His ways.

Follow God's example, therefore, as dearly loved children.

Ephesians 5:1

SPEAK, LORD, for your SERVANT is LISTENING.

1 Samuel 3:9

ires rage, winds roar, earthquakes shatter, but the Lord whispers. He whispers in the quiet stillness. His gentle whisper echoes in the soft, drowsy moments between drifting to sleep and dreaming; in the early morning, those deeply crimson moments of the rising day; and in those hushed and humbled moments when our hearts bow to heaven . . . and when heaven bends to speak.

Quench the fires of urgency, silence the winds of demands, still the quaking and trembling of this uncertain world . . . and listen. "Speak, Lord," for we, Your servants, are listening.

*T*ime . . . it trickles on, never stopping, never ceasing, marking our moments and defining our days. There are times of weeping and times of incomprehensible joy. Times of loving until our hearts burst and times of losing until our hearts ache and then break. Times of battles and times of peace, of sorrows and celebrations, of sickness and health, of dancing and solemn stillness.

And then there is God, timeless and eternal, the Maker and Master of time. He gathers all our many seasons unto Himself, transforming them into things of beauty and purpose in His own perfect time.

There is a time for EVERYTHING, AND A SEASON FOR EVERY activity UNDER THE heavens.

Ecclesiastes 3:1

CAST YOUR cares ON THE LORD & HE WILL SUSTAIN you.

PSALM 55:22

Cast your cares on the LORD and he will sustain you;
he will never let the righteous be shaken.

·······

The load is so heavy, the day is so long, and our souls grow
so weary. We cannot take one . . . more . . . step. So we
drop to our knees, fall before the Lord, and cast our cares upon
Him. We give Him all the worries, the doubts, the fears. We
give Him the endless *what-ifs* and *should haves*, the broken hearts
and broken dreams. And He takes them. He takes them all.

Then He gives. He lifts us up, strengthens us, and sustains
us. With unimaginable tenderness and indescribable love, He
takes all that we give Him, and then He gives us all that He is.

IT
IS
MORE
Blessed
TO
GIVE
THAN TO
Receive.

ACTS
20:35

In everything I did, I showed you that by this kind
of hard work we must help the weak, remembering
the words the Lord Jesus himself said: "It is more
blessed to give than to receive."

Heavenly yet humble, Jesus came not to take but to give: to give hope, to give joy, to give love. And we who choose to follow after Him are to do the same. We open our hands to give of our plenty, our hearts to give of our love. We reach out to serve those whom God has placed on our path.

We give because God gave. And we give, for in the giving we find a great gift: we experience something of the true heart, the true love of our Lord.

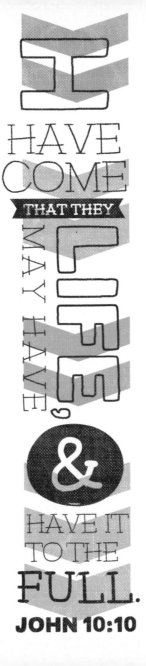

I HAVE COME THAT THEY MAY HAVE LIFE & HAVE IT TO THE FULL.

JOHN 10:10

"The thief comes only to steal and kill and destroy; I have come that they may have life, and have it to the full."

Abundant and blessed—that is the life Christ came to earth to give us. That is the life for which He sacrificed and died. He did not come to have us live in fear, to cower and timidly slip through the shadows of this life. He came to give us courage and boldness, to enable us to speak out and to reach out to a world desperately in need of Him.

So, may we cast aside fear. May we embrace the joy and hope of our Lord. And may we fan into flame the gifts with which we have been graced and live this life to abundant fullness for His glory!

*B*lessed. We who name Jesus our Savior are so very, so richly blessed. Whatever our life, whatever our lot, we are blessed. Whether in sorrow or song, whether poor or rich, whether embattled or at peace, we are blessed because we are the Lord's.

The troubles of this world will be many and they will be great, but nothing—not one thing—is greater than the goodness of our God and the love He lavishes upon us. He provides us with His salvation, gifts us with His presence, sustains us with His strength. We who are His are blessed beyond all time, beyond all price, beyond all measure.

Blessed are the poor in spirit, for theirs is the kingdom of heaven. Blessed are those who mourn, for they will be comforted. Blessed are the meek, for they will inherit the earth. Blessed are those who hunger & thirst for righteousness, for they will be filled. Blessed are the merciful, for they will be shown mercy. Blessed are the pure in heart, for they will see God. Blessed are the peacemakers, for they will be called children of God. Blessed are those who are persecuted because of righteousness, for theirs is the kingdom of heaven. –Matthew 5:3-10

Our debt is so great, we cannot repay it. God has given us so much, and only one thing does He ask for in return: *love*. We are to love the King who created us, the God who gave us His Son, the Lord who lavishes His own love upon us. We are to love Him as He loves us: unselfishly and unceasingly, without counting the cost. We are to love with all the will of our souls, all the power of our strength, with every thought of our mind.

And then He asks just one thing more of us, just one thing more we can do for Him: love one another as He loves us.

"LOVE THE LORD YOUR GOD WITH ALL YOUR HEART AND WITH ALL YOUR SOUL AND WITH ALL YOUR STRENGTH AND WITH ALL YOUR MIND;" AND, "LOVE YOUR NEIGHBOR AS YOURSELF."

LUKE 10:27

The shadows darken, the cold creeps in, and it seems that victory has been vanquished, that hope is lost . . . but no! That is not true; that is *never* true. Hold fast to hope! Hold fast to the Lord!

In His hands, evil intentions are transformed into golden, gleaming opportunities for us to seek Him and for Him to save. What the world intends for harm, the Lord captures and recreates, refining it for His own purpose, His own good, great, and glorious purpose.

Evil will never triumph. Darkness will never defeat the Light. And the will of the Lord—the goodness of God—*will* be done. Always.

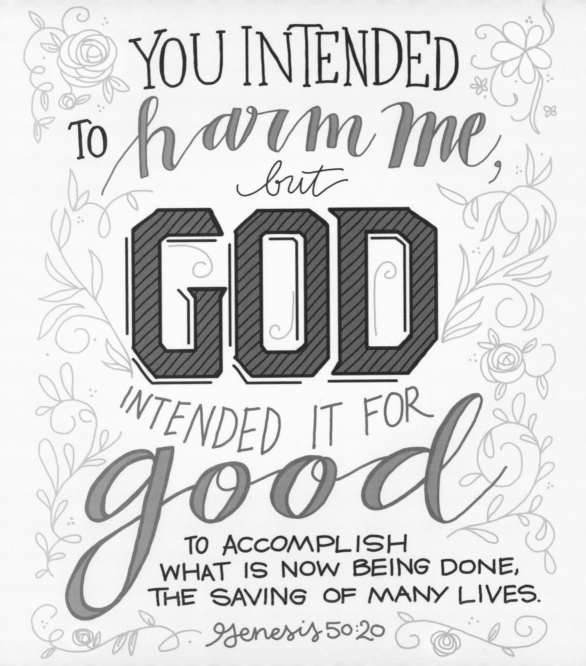

YOU INTENDED TO *harm me,* but GOD INTENDED IT FOR *good* TO ACCOMPLISH WHAT IS NOW BEING DONE, THE SAVING OF MANY LIVES. *Genesis 50:20*

You are a chosen people, a royal priesthood, a holy nation, God's special possession, that you may declare the praises of him who called you out of darkness into his wonderful light.

Chosen . . . *selected* . . . *cherished*. Those wonderful words mean that you are not an afterthought, or an *also*, or a *just another*. You who name Jesus your Savior—you are *chosen*.

Chosen by God Himself to be His very own possession, to be cherished beyond imagining, to be lifted out of darkness and lovingly cradled within the warm welcome of His wonderful light. No longer a nobody, but now part of a royal priesthood, you are called to His side.

Let our praises ring throughout the heavens and earth, calling to all who linger in darkness, "Come and know that you are chosen too."

Declare the PRAISES of HIM WHO CALLED YOU out of darkness INTO HIS wonderful LIGHT.

1 Peter 2:9

*S*orrow . . . sweet, godly sorrow . . . born of God . . . a place of—and an invitation to—grace.

Such sorrow has a place and a purpose in our lives. Sorrow moves hearts away from darkness, returns wandering minds to thoughts of Him, restores souls, and seals them for eternity.

Godly sorrow is not empty or meaningless; it is not the useless regret or guilt that prompts us to stay separated from the very One who would comfort us and restore us. Godly sorrow is a gift, a gentle nudge from our loving Shepherd to us, one of His wandering sheep. The nudge fills us with a longing to run home, to run into the waiting and welcoming arms of our Savior's grace.

Godly *sorrow* BRINGS REPENTANCE —THAT LEADS TO— SALVATION leaves NO REGRET.

2 CORINTHIANS 7:10

There are days when we turn from God, when we know right and still we choose wrong. Oh, how we need the Lord's rescue from our own stubborn waywardness! To Him, we confess our sins, the turnings of our heart, the missteps of our ways. And we wait upon His mercy, for we know and we trust that His mercy is great.

Because God's Son, our saving grace, has made a way for us, we come before the Lord with this plea: *rain down Your mercies, wash away our wickedness, cleanse us, and make us fully whole . . . fully Your own.*

Let us fall into the hands of the LORD, for his mercy is great.

2 SAMUEL 24:14

HE
WAS
PIERCED
》FOR
OUR
TRANSGRESSIONS.
HE
WAS
CRUSHED
》FOR
OUR
INIQUITIES...
BY
HIS
WOUNDS
WE
ARE
HEALED.

ISAIAH 53:5

He was pierced for our transgressions, he was crushed for our iniquities; the punishment that brought us peace was on him, and by his wounds we are healed.

The nails should have been ours, the scourge should have torn the skin on our backs, and the cross should have been ours to hang from . . . but they were not. Our destiny should have been the grave and eternal separation from God, but instead it is rich, full, and eternal life in the presence of God, our heavenly Father. All this is possible because Jesus—Son of God and heaven's own treasure—took the nails, the flogging, and the cross in our stead.

The One who was innocent and without sin took our punishment as His own. The Pure and Holy chose the defilement of death. Our transgressions, our sins, our falling short of God's standards—for those Jesus was pierced and His lifeblood poured out. And by His wounds—by His love—we are healed.

Jesus looked at [his disciples] and said, "With man this is impossible, but with God all things are possible."

———— ◦ ————

Hopeless. Purposeless. Alone. Such is the destiny of people without God.

Hope-filled. Purposeful. Adopted. Such is the reality of people who love God, for whom nothing is impossible.

What great joy that we who are His children need never be without God. The impossible was made possible: sinners are forgiven by God and welcomed into His forever family, by His might, power, and grace. Gifted with hope, we find purpose in life, meaning in struggles, and possibility in the face of the impossible.

For nothing—not one single thing—is impossible for our Lord. No hurt is beyond His healing touch, no need is too great for His resources, and no soul is past saving. For with God all things are made possible.

with man this is impossible, but with God all things are possible.

Matthew 19:26

A life well lived is a life of joy and peace; of laughter and, yes, tears; a life of patience, of purpose, of hope.

A life well lived is a life that loves openly and gives generously, that does not demand power and control, that is not afraid to be gentle and kind even to those who are not.

And a life well lived is a life that willingly sets aside selfish ambitions and instead offers up a thousand tiny, daily sacrifices of self.

What is this life well lived? It is a life lived with, and in, and for Christ.

Above all else, guard your heart, for everything you do flows from it.

Proverbs 4:23

From the heart flow our dreams, our passions, our ideals. Its depths form the wellspring of all our thoughts, words, and actions. When we yield our hearts to God and they become filled with the glorious riches of Christ, they pour forth love, hope, and joy, bringing Him great glory. But empty of Christ, a heart stands vulnerable to darkness.

And so we guard the heart above all else. We secure it within God's fortress of grace, fortify it with prayers, and seal it with His praises. And because all our thoughts, words, and actions flow from the heart, we open our hearts to God, that His love will flow through us.

PEOPLE
LOOK
♥ AT THE
outward
APPEARANCE,
but
the LORD
looks at the
heart.
1 SAMUEL 16:7

The LORD said to Samuel, "Do not consider his appearance
or his height, for I have rejected him. The LORD does not
look at the things people look at. People look at the outward
appearance, but the LORD looks at the heart."

Open our eyes, Lord. Open our eyes to see as You see so
that we may give as You give, love as You love.
Do not let our eyes be led astray, deceived by grandeur, glitz,
or glamour. Let us see truth. And teach us to see possibilities
instead of poverty, to give grace instead of judgment, and
to remember that all people—*all* people—are Your precious
creations, made to love and to be loved . . . without fear,
without reservation, without holding back.

Is anything too difficult for God? For He who has poured out the oceans and measured their waters in the hollow of His hand? He is the Master of mountains and the Carver of canyons. With outstretched arms, He flung the stars, sparkling and bright, into the darkness of the heavens. Nothing—no, nothing—is too difficult for our great God!

And yet, He kneels down from the heights of the heavens. The One who calls the stars by name also calls each of us by name. With outstretched arms, He pulls us close, cradling us near His heart. For nothing is too great for our God.

AH, *Sovereign Lord,*

you have made the HEAVENS and the EARTH by your *great power* and OUTSTRETCHED ARM. NOTHING *is too hard for* YOU.

JEREMIAH 32:17

WHOEVER
— DOES NOT —
CARRY
THEIR CROSS

FOLLOW ME
— CANNOT BE —
MY
DISCIPLE.

Luke 14:27

The cross on which Christ hung stood on a hill, steeped in sin, stained crimson with His blood. Heaven's greatest sorrow, and our greatest joy. Victory over sin, over death.

And for those who follow Him, a cross awaits. Not a cross of wood. Not fashioned by Roman hands. But our greatest struggle—our cross—leading us to Him, our greatest joy.

Christ bore His cross alone and in darkness, but we? We do not labor alone. Nail-scarred hands cover ours, bloodied shoulders bear our burden, carrying our cross, carrying us as we walk with Him.

No temptation has overtaken you except what is common to mankind. And God is faithful; he will not let you be tempted beyond what you can bear. But when you are tempted, he will also provide a way out so that you can endure it.

Our Savior walked where we walk, faced the fallen world we face, and still He stood firm.

And when we turn to Him, He empowers us to stand strong. There is no darkness His light cannot penetrate, no depth of despair from which He cannot rescue, no temptation beyond His power to vanquish. He does not leave us to stumble, lost and alone.

Instead, He promises strength for our weakness and sight for our blindness. When we struggle in the murky mire of temptation, He clears away the debris of distraction and sin, and He whispers, *This way.*

God

is FAITHFUL;

HE

will

N o t

let

YOU

BE

tempted

BEYOND

WHAT

you

C A N

bear.

I CORINTHIANS 10:13

"See, I am doing a new thing! Now it springs up; do you not perceive it? I am making a way in the wilderness and streams in the wasteland."

Let go! May we let go of the past, of the failings of our old ways, and then take hold of the truth of Christ. For He offers new life: He wants to do a new thing in us and with us and through us. The Lord God of heaven calls to us by name, for we are His.

Waters of evil threaten to engulf us, yet we pass through them unharmed. Flames of life's challenges and losses blaze around us, but we are not burned, for the Lord is our Shield and our Defender. And He who made a way through the raging sea has made a way for us.

ALL SCRIPTURE IS GOD-BREATHED AND IS USEFUL FOR TEACHING. 2 TIMOTHY 3:16

All Scripture is God-breathed and is useful for teaching, rebuking, correcting and training in righteousness.

The life-giving breath of God makes His Word alive. From its pages we, in turn, draw in its life-giving power, letting it fill us, make us, mold us. Scripture's strength is our tower of refuge; its power is our shield and our hope; its promises are our souls' salvation.

Breathless and hurting, weary and wandering, we hunger for the bread of righteousness, we thirst for the living waters, we seek the rest and redemption that Scripture provides. Whenever we open the Word, the Spirit Himself fills us with light, with life, with the very breath of God.

Walls of stone, fences of hatred, words that divide and destroy—these boundaries both define and separate, creating an *us* and a *them*.

But there is no separation between Christ and us. There is only love—sweet, pure, and unending, yet able to blast through walls, break down fences, and heal the deepest of wounds.

The devil may rant and rage, but his powers of hatred wither and pale in the brilliant light of Christ's love. For nothing—*nothing!*—can ever separate those of us who love Christ from the love He has for us.

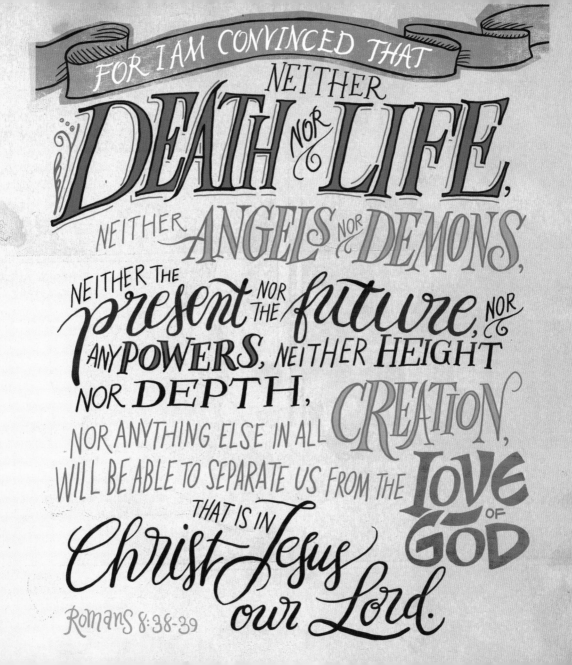

FOR I AM CONVINCED THAT NEITHER DEATH NOR LIFE, NEITHER ANGELS NOR DEMONS, NEITHER THE present NOR THE future, NOR ANY POWERS, NEITHER HEIGHT NOR DEPTH, NOR ANYTHING ELSE IN ALL CREATION, WILL BE ABLE TO SEPARATE US FROM THE LOVE OF GOD THAT IS IN Christ Jesus our Lord.

Romans 8:38-39

It's one single step, slow, faltering, and uncertain, as doubts weigh heavy and ghosts of past sins haunt and trouble. But still we step, daring to hope for a new beginning, daring to draw just a little nearer, our heart seeking a home, and . . . then?

And then the wondrous welcome as the Father rushes toward us, arms stretched wide, sweeping us into His loving embrace. Prodigal hearts forgiven and pressed close to His. Seeking, suffering souls welcomed home. And it begins—always begins—when we take a single step, just one step toward Him.

COME
NEAR TO
God
and
HE WILL
COME NEAR TO
you.
JAMES 4:8

Even youths grow tired and weary, and young men stumble and fall; but those who hope in the LORD will renew their strength. They will soar on wings like eagles; they will run and not grow weary, they will walk and not be faint.

To live with Christ is to lift stumbling feet from the miry clay of duties and demands, to be freed from the shackles of this earthbound life, and to shake off burdens and sorrows. It is to soar on wings as strong as the eagle's.

Impossible? No! It is possible because it is *promised* by God to those who believe, those who trust, those who dare to step to the edge of the cliff of faith and leap—flying, not falling, into the Father's arms. No weariness, no fear, no despair. Just simple soaring . . . beautiful, joyful, joy-filled soaring with our Savior.

They will SOAR on wings like EAGLES; THEY WILL RUN and not grow weary, THEY WILL WALK and not be faint.

Isaiah 40:30-31

May
THESE WORDS
of my
MOUTH
and
THIS
MEDITATION
of my
HEART
be.
pleasing
IN YOUR
SIGHT.

PSALM 19:14

May these words of my mouth and this meditation of my heart be pleasing in your sight, LORD, my Rock and my Redeemer.

How often we fail Him and fall before Him, pleading for mercy, for forgiveness, for blamelessness in His eyes. So, we pore over the precepts of His Word, inscribing its truth upon our hearts, engraving it on our minds. More luminous than gold, sweeter than honey, God's Word gives light to our paths, peace to our present, and promise to our future. As we allow Truth to transform us, we replace words that tear down with words that give life.

May our every thought—and may every word that tumbles from our lips—be pleasing to the Lord, our Rock and our Redeemer.

What must I do to be saved?" (Acts 16:30). This question cried out centuries ago still echoes today. And the answer, the beautiful answer, remains ever the same: "Believe!"

Set aside doubts, turn away from darkness, open your heart and mind to the One who offers salvation—for today, for tomorrow, for eternity—to all who believe, who follow, who obey.

Stepping out in faith and daring to embrace it changes the course of our eternities and will leave a rich legacy for our loved ones—a legacy of trusting, of hoping, of believing. Therefore . . .

"Believe!"

believe
in the
Lord
Jesus,
and you
will be
saved—
you and
your
household.

ACTS 16:31

Anxious and impatient, weary of waiting—too often
that is our way. "Hurry! Hurry!" is the cry of our rush-
and-tumble lives. We simply have no time for *time*, no patience
for *patience*.

The world seems tempest tossed, darkness surrounds us, and
we long for, pray for, beg for the Almighty to make all things
new. But our God does not hurry. Why? Because He waits
for the perfection of His eternal purpose: for His people—for
all people—to be *His* people. Oh, how He longs for all people
to know Him as Savior! For our God is love, ever knocking,
offering, calling, "Come to Me! I am waiting for *you*."

The Lord is not slow in *keeping his promise*

2 PETER 3:9

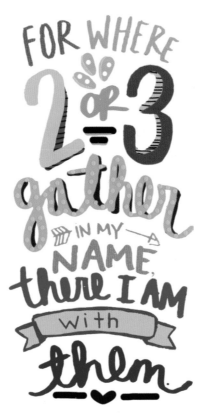

FOR WHERE
2 or 3
gather
IN MY
NAME,
there I AM
with
them.

MATTHEW 18:20

When we who are children of God and heirs of heaven gather together, power is in our midst. A power not of ourselves, but the power of God, the Almighty, *Elohim*.

For when we, the purchased children of His heart, call upon His name and unite in prayer, in praise, in purpose, then the Lord Himself steps into our midst, encourages us with His presence, and fills us with His own strong and mighty Holy Spirit. And we are blessed and He is glorified as we lift our concerns to our ever-faithful God.

the

fear

of the Lord is
the beginning of

wisdom,

and knowledge
of the

Holy One

is understanding.

**Proverbs
9:10**

The fear of the Lord—our acknowledgment of His holiness, His power, His love—is the beginning of our journey, it is every step along the path, and it is the end.

To fear God is to walk in His ways, to follow His teachings. It is loving and serving Him and others with all that we are and all that we ever hope to be. To fear the Lord—to know Him and to honor Him—gives us our first glimmer of wisdom and fuels our first trembling tread on our journey to understanding. For salvation begins with our fear of the Lord.

To give, for we have been given much; to bless, for innumerable are the blessings we have received—*this* the Lord asks of us. And He gives specifics: set aside words of anger, bitterness, and strife, and instead offer words of kindness and compassion. Words that heal and offer hope. Words that acknowledge we are not so different, that all of us are seekers searching for home, all sinners in need of saving grace.

So, when the world strikes and our cheek feels the sting, we turn and we forgive. By doing so, we give the gift that we ourselves have been given.

Be & kind compassionate to 1 another, forgiving each other, just as in Christ God forgave you.

Ephesians 4:32

"I have told you these things, so that in me you may have peace. In this world you will have trouble. But take heart! I have overcome the world."

The enemy seems to surround us; he troubles us and threatens us, but we do not give up nor do we stand alone. Like the trumpeting warriors of old, we boldly call upon the name of our God—our Rock and Shield and Defender—and He stands with us.

The enemy may rage and roar. Yes, the battle continues even after Jesus' death—but the war is already won, for death could not hold Jesus! Sin was slain upon the cross, death buried in a tomb. Christ has overcome the world, and peace—soul-sealing peace—is ours to claim.

but
take
heart!
I have
over-
come
the
world!

John 16:33

I heard the voice of the Lord saying, "Whom shall I send? And who will go for us?" And I said, "Here am I. Send me!"

News of grace! News of hope! Good and wonderful and ours to share with a world hurting and hungry to hear such news—the good news of God.

But who will go? Who will tell? Who will show a lost world the way of salvation? Whose feet will carry peace into a world of discord and distress—the gospel of sweet, redeeming peace? Will we? Will we set aside worry and fear? Will *we* go?

Give us Your courage, Your strength, and we will be Your hands, Your feet, in this world that needs Your love. Here are we! Send us!

Only the Lamb of God is worthy of all honor and glory and praise. Only the Lamb, pure and perfect, would take our place, take our sins, take our death—and then clothe us in His righteousness, in His life-giving salvation. *Only the Lamb.*

Let every creature that draws breath in heaven and on earth and under the earth and in the sea, let all proclaim that the Lamb is worthy. And let our hearts, our very souls, cry out His praises for all time. Only the Lamb is worthy! Only the Lamb is Lord and King!

Worthy is the Lamb, who was slain, to receive power & wealth & wisdom & strength & honor & glory & praise!

Revelation 5:12

At all times, in all ways, and in all things, we whisper the prayers of our hearts to heaven. With words, without words, with deepest groanings of the Spirit within us, we turn to the One who always hears us.

Times of joy float up to our Father on wings of laughter and with shouts of praise. Times of sadness and sorrow are lifted up with trembling hands and placed carefully, so carefully, within His tender keeping.

Ever seeking, ever finding . . . always we pray, always we give thanks, and always the Father listens.

Pray continually,
give thanks in
all circumstances;
for this is God's
will for you in
Christ Jesus.

1 Thessalonians 5:17-18

So we fix our eyes not on what is seen, but on what is unseen,
since what is seen is temporary, but what is unseen is eternal.

Difficult days and trying times—such is the world we live in. As the apostle Paul put it, "We are hard pressed on every side, but not crushed; perplexed, but not in despair; persecuted, but not abandoned; struck down, but not destroyed" (2 Corinthians 4:8–9). Instead, we have hope because we belong to the Lord.

Though we do not see Jesus' face, touch His hand, or hear His voice, He is more real than any mountain; His presence is more certain than the sea. He is like the wind: unseen, yet touching all, stirring all, impacting all. So we keep our eyes ever fixed on Him.

SO WE *fix* OUR

EYES

NOT ON

what is seen,

BUT ON

WHAT

IS

unseen.

2 CORINTHIANS 4:18

We can do *all* things through the power of our Lord. Alone, we are but wandering sheep, weak and vulnerable, stumbling, lost, and purposeless. But with and empowered by the Lord, our God and our Shepherd, we are strong, we are protected, we are guided, and we live with *divine* purpose.

Our way through this world will be marked with troubles, temptations, and trials. But we can know joy, and we can know peace. For our strength comes not from within ourselves and not from the world. Our strength comes from the Lord, the God of all.

EVERYONE WHO CALLS on the NAME of the Lord WILL BE SAVED.

ROMANS 10:13

*G*race—the glorious and God-given grace of sins forgiven and relationship with Jesus made possible—this grace is offered to all. Freely given to any who will receive, who will proclaim, the name of Jesus, and any who will follow Him. In Christ, through Christ, we are richly blessed, graciously saved.

The love of Jesus knows no national borders, no boundaries of wealth, no color of skin: all—*all*—are precious to Him. There is no separation, no segregation, no *us* or *them* for those who call upon His name, who kneel at His cross, who are cleansed by His blood. There are only those who are His.

Each of you should use whatever gift you have received to serve others, as faithful stewards of God's grace in its various forms.

❧

It is a gift, priceless and true, this thing that God has given each of us the ability to do. It is a gift, not to squander or neglect, but to use. Not for personal glory or selfish gain, but for God, for His kingdom, and because of His love.

The gift is ours both to keep and to give, to use to bless others as we've been blessed by God. For whatever our gift—whatever that beautiful, shining ability, trait, or passion inside each of us—may be, it is given to us to serve God and His people, to use for God's glory, to point others to Him, the Giver of gifts.

Each of
you should
use whatever
gift you have
received to
serve others.

1 Peter 4:10

there
will be
no more
death
or
mourning
or
crying
or
pain.

REVELATION 21:4

*He will wipe every tear from their eyes. There will be no
more death or mourning or crying or pain, for the old
order of things has passed away.*

Heaven will be a new beginning, as beautiful as a bride, fresh
and shining, bright with hope, with love, with joy.

This glorious new beginning is also an end. An end to
sadness and sorrow, an end to longing and loss, an end to
broken hopes and broken hearts.

Heaven is kneeling before the throne of God, seeing His
face, and feeling the touch of His fingers as He gently wipes
away the last tear, the last trace of sorrow. Heaven is living
with our Lord in light, in love, and in peace . . . for always.

The opportunity is ours. Each day, each moment, is our gift from God: the gift of life, the gift of freedom, the gift of choice. We can choose our direction and our focus; we can choose to see His hand and His handiwork. Evil would darken our hearts and minds, seeking to shut out the Savior. But we can choose not to miss the evidence of His goodness, a light that shatters darkness.

We can choose the sun's bright rays over the storm. We can choose kindness and truth. We can choose righteousness and excellence. We can choose beauty and purity.

In choosing the good, we choose God.

FINALLY, BROTHERS & SISTERS, WHATEVER IS TRUE, WHATEVER IS NOBLE, WHATEVER IS RIGHT, WHATEVER IS PURE, WHATEVER IS LOVELY, WHATEVER IS ADMIRABLE— IF ANYTHING IS EXCELLENT OR PRAISEWORTHY— THINK ABOUT SUCH THINGS.

PHILIPPIANS 4:8

*C*ome."

When the world wearies, steals joy, and drowns hope, when the battles have been too fierce and too long, do we accept the Lord's invitation to *come* to Him? With burdens too heavy for us to carry alone, we can fall at His feet, and He will lift us up. And in Him we may find rest—sweet rest that restores hurting hearts, bruised and battered souls, and weary spirits.

When we linger in His presence and breathe in His peace, we will find renewal and refreshment in the rest He gives.

Come to me,
all you who are weary and burdened,
and I will give you rest.

Matthew 11:28

AND WE KNOW THAT IN ALL THINGS GOD WORKS FOR THE GOOD OF THOSE WHO LOVE HIM, WHO HAVE BEEN CALLED ACCORDING TO HIS PURPOSE.

ROMANS 8:28

The fabric of our lives stretches before us, and we see the threads of broken dreams, the gaping holes rendered by loss, and the fraying edges of struggles with health, with home, with hope. But the Lord sees more. His hands are always working on the tapestry of our lives, restoring, revealing purpose and meaning, creating beauty.

Heavenly fingers, sure and certain, weave broken dreams into brilliant new realities, transform gaping holes into an iron-strong lacework of life-tested faith, and mend fraying edges, smoothing them into softness by His grace. For all things are made beautiful by the touch of God's hand.

*"Look, I am coming soon! My reward is with me,
and I will give to each person according to what they
have done."*

Who is coming? Our God and King, our Savior and Friend. The One who—in His own words—is Alpha and Omega, the Beginning and the End. The Lord, the great and mighty Jehovah, is coming soon. And He is coming upon the clouds to claim us, His chosen children.

Merciful to those who call upon His name, Jesus remembers not the sins of our youth, not the rebelliousness of our hearts. No, the tattered and filthy rags of our sins have been stripped away, and we are clothed in brilliant, shining robes of righteousness. Of Jesus' righteousness credited to us. And this Jesus, our Rock, our Rescuer, our Redeemer—He is coming! *Lord, come quickly!*

About the Artists

Juicebox Designs is an award-winning graphic design firm in Nashville, Tennessee, owned by the husband-and-wife team of Jay and Kristi Smith. They specialize in carefully crafted design, illustration, and hand-lettering for their clients and their line of retail products. For more information on Juicebox Designs and to see their design work, visit juiceboxdesigns.com. Find their work on pages 13, 14, 25, 37, 50, 55, 76, 80, 103, 105, 117, 120, 123, 133, 135, 137, 147, 150, 153, 160, 163, 167, 168, 171, 181, 189, 196.

Kerri Charlton studied graphic design and illustration at Texas Tech University. Her hobbies are still the same after forty years: drawing, coloring, playing outside, reading, and taking naps. She is married to a helicopter pilot. Find her work on pages 9, 19, 28, 33, 35, 44, 47, 56, 59, 72, 85, 97, 100, 109, 110, 115, 126, 145, 158, 176, 199, 201, 202.

Shanna Noel is the founder of Illustrated Faith. A wife and mother of two, Shanna is a lifelong scrapbooker who started using her passion and a journaling Bible to begin illustrating her faith. Her creative ideas for Bible journaling help women and men connect with God's Word in amazing new ways. Find her work on pages 10, 16, 30, 38, 53, 60, 64, 79, 86, 107, 119, 124, 139, 148, 154, 165, 174, 182, 185, 191, 192, 195.

Micah Kandros is an award-winning designer and photographer. For more than fifteen years, he has been designing book covers for *New York Times* bestselling authors, branding new publishing ventures, photographing celebrities and country music stars, and working on major print campaigns for universities. Find his work on pages 20, 43, 68, 75, 91, 95, 112, 128, 141, 142, 179.

Megan Wells is a South Florida artist inspired by beautiful words and God's creation. Her work combines whimsical florals with flowing letterforms. When not busy creating in her studio, you can find her riding bikes to the beach with her husband, Brent, playing tennis, or sipping coffee. Learn more at makewells.com. Find her work on pages 7, 27, 49, 63, 83, 99, 187, 205.

Tiffany Zajas is a hand-lettering and illustration artist who loves using creativity to bring life and joy to others. She lives in Nashville, Tennessee, with her husband and two little boys (with another baby on the way). To see more of what Tiffany is up to, visit tiffanyzajas.com or @tiffanyzajas on Instagram. Find her work on pages 23, 67, 71, 88, 92, 131.

Jasmine Jones is a graphic designer and artist who specializes in floral designs and hand-lettering. Her illustrations can be found on products in the paper crafting, gift, and home goods industries. When she's not creating art, she enjoys perusing junk shops, trying new restaurants, and watching old movies. You can find more at jasminenorajones.com. Find her work on pages 40, 157, 173.